Maya ANGELOU

Biography

Maya ANGELOU

by L. Patricia Kite

Lerner Publications Company
Minneapolis

This book is dedicated to my wonderful daughter, Sally Susannah Kite, who has always helped me work toward being a success in life. And with very special thanks to my friend, Jean Powell Ficklin, founder of our Afro-American Cultural & Historical Society

A&E and **BIOGRAPHY** are trademarks of the A&E Television Networks, registered in the United States and other countries.

Some of the people profiled in this series have also been featured in A&E's acclaimed BIOGRAPHY series, which is available on videocassete from A&E Home Video. Call 1-800-423-1212 to order.

Lerner Publications Company
241 First Avenue North
Minneapolis, MN 55401

Website address: www.lernerbooks.com

Library of Congress Cataloging-in-Publication Data

Kite, L. Patricia
    Maya Angelou / L. Patricia Kite.
        p.   cm. — (A & E biography)
    Includes bibliographical references (p.   ) and index.
    Summary: A biography of the multi-faceted African-American woman.
Maya Angelou, tracing her life from her childhood in the segregated
South to her prominence as a well-known writer.
    ISBN 0-8225-4944-1 (alk. Paper)
    1. Angelou, Maya—Biography—Juvenile literature. 2. Afro-
American women authors—20th century—Biography—Juvenile
literature.   [1. Angelou, Maya. 2. Authors, American. 3. Afro-
Americans—Biography. 4. Women—Biography.] I. Title.
II. Series.
PS3551.N454M39   1999
818'.5409-dc21
[B]   98-15763

Manufactured in the United States of America
1 2 3 4 5 6 – JR – 04 03 02 01 00 99

CONTENTS

Maya Angelou reads her poem "On the Pulse of Morning" at President Bill Clinton's inauguration on January 20, 1993.

Chapter ONE

POET FOR A PRESIDENT

OUTSIDE MAYA ANGELOU'S SPACIOUS, REDBRICK colonial home in Winston-Salem, North Carolina, the skies were gray and threatened rain, yet it was warm and cozy inside. Maya lounged in a green velvet chair, talking to one of the many reporters and magazine journalists who had requested interviews. So many people wanted to know why president-elect Bill Clinton requested that she recite her poetry at his inaugural ceremony. No poet had been invited to participate in an inaugural since Robert Frost recited "The Gift Outright" at John F. Kennedy's inauguration in 1961.

Certainly Maya's 50 honorary degrees, her best-selling poetry and autobiographical books, and her outstanding work in the black and world communities were compelling factors. Perhaps Clinton felt a special kinship because he was born in a small town called Hope, Arkansas, just 25 miles from Maya's rural childhood home in Stamps, Arkansas. Or perhaps there were other, more important factors. "He knows my work," Maya clarified, emphasizing that Bill Clinton reads poetry, and poetry is a universal language.

When working, Maya usually researches and writes about 16 hours a day, but it's always been difficult for her to write at home. Each lovely room, replete with African sculptures and African-American art, is filled with memories that distract her from the task at hand. To solve that problem, Maya rents a tiny hotel room. Waking about 4:00 A.M., she goes to the hotel about 7:00 A.M. and works at least six hours, although that schedule became difficult to maintain after being put in the spotlight of Clinton's invitation. In the hotel room, Maya keeps a dictionary, a thesaurus, a Bible, and a pack of cards. An occasional game of solitaire keeps her hands busy while she thinks. There's a bed in the room, but she never rests on it.

Maya writes longhand with a pen on lined, yellow legal pads. Sometimes her eyelids swell closed from fatigue and her back aches. At 64, her arthritis is bothersome. Decades of writing for hours at a time have taken their toll. In preparation for the inauguration, she had been working seven days a week. Sometimes, while writing, Maya prays. Sometimes she sings.

Pressure to select a topic for the inaugural poem was

Maya sometimes plays a game of solitaire while she is thinking.

enormous. Maya received 1200 letters per week, and the telephone rang constantly. Everywhere, people stopped her to offer their ideas and commentary. Women of all colors and identities wanted to be heard. Black people wanted their story told. White people urged her to use words that would stop racial division.

Maya mentioned to a reporter that the president-elect may have asked her to write an inaugural poem because he realized Maya's gift of bringing people together and incorporating into her work the concept that human beings are more alike than they are different. She believes poetry is strength for the spirit. It can inspire an entire country.

On January 20, 1993, Bill Clinton became the 42nd president of the United States. On the steps of the Capitol, at least 250,000 people watched the ceremony, while waving flags and cheering. Standing next to the new president, Maya Angelou became the first black woman to recite her poetry at a U.S. presidential inauguration. She called her poem "On the Pulse of Morning."

When Maya and her brother moved to Stamps, Arkansas, black people had to live in a separate section of town.

Chapter **TWO**

ARRIVING IN STAMPS, ARKANSAS

MAYA ANGELOU WAS BORN MARGUERITE ANNIE Johnson in St. Louis, Missouri, on April 4, 1928. Her mother, Vivian Baxter Johnson, was working as a card dealer. Maya's father, Bailey Johnson, was a hotel doorman. She had a brother, Bailey Jr., who was one year older than Maya.

That same year, the Johnson family moved to Long Beach, California. Once there, toddler Bailey Jr. decided the name "Marguerite" was too long and difficult to pronounce. Instead, he called her "Mya Sister," which gradually became "Maya."

In 1931, when Maya was three years old, her parents got a divorce. A year later, Bailey Sr. sent the two children to live with his mother, Annie Henderson, in the small town of Stamps, Arkansas. Maya and Bailey Jr. boarded the train alone, wearing identification tags on their wrists. The tags read "To Whom It May Concern" and stated the children were Marguerite and Bailey Johnson Jr., traveling from Long Beach to Stamps, c/o Mrs. Annie Henderson.

When Maya and Bailey arrived in Stamps, they found an economically depressed town. Stamps was also a segregated community. Black residents lived in one area, called the "Quarters," and white residents lived in another. The railroad tracks and the Red River divided the two areas. Within the Quarters, most of the men earned a living by dirt farming. The women helped work the land and took in washing and ironing. Some black people worked on the large cotton plantations owned by white people. Others—except Annie Henderson—worked in the houses of white people.

Maya and Bailey called their grandmother "Momma." She stood 6 feet 2 inches tall, and her skin was cinnamon colored. She was a big-boned woman with a wide face, high cheekbones, and slanted eyes.

Twenty-eight years earlier, after an unhappy marriage, her husband, William Johnson, had left Momma Annie to become a preacher in Oklahoma. He took what little money they had, leaving Momma with their two young sons, Bailey and Willie, and the one-room house in Stamps.

Momma Annie did not want to go to work in a white person's home, leaving her two little boys in someone else's care. She could only read a bit and do a little math, but one skill she definitely had was cooking tasty, stomach-filling meals.

Keeping her plans secret, Momma Annie tested her physical strength by spending one entire evening carrying heavy pails of stones on a 16-mile round-trip to the local cotton gin and lumber mill. Knowing she could carry heavy loads for long distances, she worked until early morning, frying ham and boiling chickens. Then she made many meat pies, which she carried, along with an iron brazier—a pan for holding burning coals—to the cotton gin. When she arrived, she warmed the pies, which created a tempting aroma. Momma Annie offered cold lemonade and delicious meat pies to the workers for just five cents each. Soon she was selling homemade meals to workers at the local lumber mill, too.

For the next few years, regardless of the weather, Annie Henderson carried her iron brazier to the work sites. When satisfied that she had a regular customer base, she built a stall, or food stand, between the two work centers, encouraging the workers to come to her.

In time, the stall became the Wm. Johnson General Merchandise Store, a place where the black residents of Stamps could buy what they needed. If Momma Annie didn't have an item in stock, she would order it. The Store, always referred to with a capital S, gradually became the center of the black residents' activities.

In the 1930s, many black men worked on cotton plantations owned by white people.

Chapter THREE

Momma and the Store

AFTER WILLIAM JOHNSON LEFT HER, MOMMA Annie married a Mr. Henderson and later a Mr. Murphy, but she was no longer married when Maya and Bailey Jr. arrived in 1931. Momma Annie ran the Store with her son Willie. Willie was paralyzed on his right side. He was a big man who walked with difficulty, leaning on a cane.

Willie, Momma, Maya, and Bailey lived in the back portion of the Store, but the children spent much of their time in the front. It became Maya's favorite place, because every black person in Stamps visited at one time or another. The children helped Momma ladle out flour, corn, sugar, and mash, or grain meal, putting the purchases in thin paper sacks. When the weather was nice, the local barber set up shop outside the Store, giving haircuts on the front porch.

In the evening, the children helped feed the livestock. They threw corn to the chickens and mixed sour mash—or steeped grain meal—with leftover food and dishwater to make swill for the pigs. Maya and Bailey often stayed to hear the pigs' contented grunting. Sometimes the children playfully grunted back. Maya enjoyed just about anything she did with Bailey. Not only did she think he was the best person in the whole world, she also thought he was the most handsome. Bailey's skin was "velvet-black," his hair was curly, and he had a ready retort for everything.

Momma, Willie, Maya and Bailey were one of the few black families in Stamps that were not on wel-

Maya's grandmother owned and ran a general store in the heart of the black section of Stamps.

fare. The Great Depression of the 1930s affected almost the whole country and made earning a living even more difficult in places like Stamps. Families living on small farms could no longer afford food for their hogs and chickens, and food provided by welfare was the only thing that kept many people from starvation. What families didn't need, they brought to the Store to exchange for materials they could use.

From the window of the Store, Maya watched large wagons arrive to transport black men to the cotton farms of white people. Cotton picking was backbreaking work, but in the morning, the men would be optimistic about picking enough cotton to buy food for their families and pay some of their bills.

Cotton pickers worked long hours for little pay.

Black cotton pickers watch as a white overseer weighs the results of their labor.

By evening, when the men returned to the Store, they dragged their empty cotton sacks and were covered with dust. Their pay depended on the amount of cotton they picked, and they often felt cheated by irregular and unfair weighing practices. Maya watched this scene day after day, forming a mental picture she would remember all her life.

But the children did well under the watchful eyes of Momma and Uncle Willie. Momma was a stickler for cleanliness. Every evening, even in winter, Momma made Maya and Bailey go to the well and wash their faces, necks, arms, and legs. Then—except for Saturday nights—they had to do their schoolwork. On Saturday nights, they memorized their Sunday-school lesson. And, of course, there were always prayers.

In addition to running the Store and caring for the children, Momma made all of Maya's and Bailey's clothes. Maya sometimes thought she looked like "walking wallpaper," since Momma used the same material for much of the clothing. Although the children wore shoes during the winter, in summer Maya and Bailey went barefoot—except on Sundays.

On Sundays, they attended the Christian Methodist Episcopal church for black people. Momma was an

Maya and most other black children spent several hours at church on Sundays.

honored Mother of the Church, and Uncle Willie was superintendent of the Sunday School. Before church, Momma made a special breakfast of eggs, fried potatoes and onions, yellow hominy and perch fried crispy, and biscuits covered with butter.

During the six-hour church service, Maya and Bailey had to sit on hard wooden benches in the children's section. If Maya got bored during the long service, she tuned it out. She became very good at not hearing what she didn't want to hear and quite skilled at listening intently when she heard something she wanted to hear. Her favorite part of the service was the poetry of the gospel songs and spirituals.

After church and on other evenings, the family ate a big dinner, which might include tomato preserves on buttered biscuits, fried corn cakes, pork sausage, green beans, and homegrown fruit.

Whether at meals, church services, or at the Store, Momma was strict about manners. Adults had to be addressed with a respectful title, such as missus, mister, auntie, uncle, brother, bro, buddy, bubba, sister, or tutta. Titles often indicated a family relationship.

The use of titles denoting respect dated back to slavery days. After being brought to this country, slaves were given names at the whims of slave owners. Although the slaves, under penalty of severe punishment or death, couldn't do much about their names, within their own society, respectful titles were added. There was logic to the system. Children, it was felt, needed a "shelter," someone to turn to if they had a problem. If a child addressed an adult as "John" or "Mary," the name suggested that the adult was equal to the child, not someone the child could turn to for help.

However, none of these rules applied to white people, called "whitefolks." Momma taught Maya and Bailey that speaking to whitefolks at all, even politely, could mean risking their lives in that racially segregated society. In truth, black children in the Quarters did not see many white people in their daily life. Months might go by before they saw a white business person or affluent homeowner.

On occasion, the children saw white sharecroppers— people who worked land owned by another person in return for a place to live and a certain share of the crops that were grown. The white sharecroppers were sometimes called "powhitetrash," poor white trash, by both white and black people—although not to their faces. Sharecroppers earned as little as the black residents, and they were usually uneducated and did not have a strong family system. Nevertheless, the white sharecroppers, like the more affluent whites, regarded black people as their inferiors.

For Maya and her brother, life in the bustling city of St. Louis, Missouri, presented quite a change from the quiet town of Stamps, Arkansas.

Chapter FOUR

LIFE IN
ST. LOUIS

MAYA AND BAILEY DIDN'T THINK ABOUT THEIR
birth parents, since they had never heard from or
about either of them. Maya believed both parents
were dead. She sometimes pictured her mother lying
in a coffin, covered with a sheet, her black hair spread
out on a small white pillow. Since Maya didn't remember what her mother actually looked like, she
pictured her face as a brown O with the word
MOTHER imprinted on it.

Then, when Maya was six years old, she and Bailey
received Christmas gifts from both parents. Father sent
a photograph of himself, and Mother sent Maya a tea
set and a doll with blue eyes and blond hair painted
on her head. Both Maya and Bailey went outside and

cried after receiving the presents. If their parents were alive, the children wondered why they had been sent away. What terrible thing had they done?

A year later, a stranger drove up to the Store. He was a big, handsome man, soon introduced as Maya's and Bailey's father. Bailey Sr. had come to take the children back to St. Louis, Missouri, to live with their mother. Maya thought her father talked differently than the black men in Stamps. He sounded just like a white man, and she wondered if he was the only "brown-skinned white man" in the world.

As she and Bailey drove along in Father's gray De Soto car, Maya began to cry. She wanted to return to Stamps. The children were afraid to meet the woman who was their mother. What if she laughed at them?

But both Maya and Bailey Jr. loved Mother immediately. She was light skinned, five feet four inches tall, and the prettiest, liveliest woman they had ever seen. Maya seemed almost opposite in appearance. Maya's self description was a "too big Negro girl, with nappy black hair," "broad feet," and a big space between her two front teeth.

Initially the children lived with Mother's mother, Grandmother Baxter, and Father returned to California. Grandmother Baxter had skin as white as any white person, and she spoke with a German accent, since she had been raised by a German family in Illinois. She had moved to St. Louis to study nursing. While working at the local hospital, she'd met her husband, who was black. Together they had Vivian (Maya's mother) and four sons, each with a reputation for being quick tempered, tough, and mean.

St. Louis was quite different than the small farming community of Stamps. Imaginative Maya soon thought of it as a foreign country. It had many paved streets and large brick buildings, and coal dust filled the air. Buses, cars, and trucks constantly moved back and forth.

The schools in St. Louis were different too. They were much larger than even the white schools in Stamps. Maya and Bailey enrolled in Toussaint L'Ouverture Grammar School. They had been well trained by Momma and Uncle Willie in math and reading and thought their schoolmates were rather backward. They also decided their teachers were snobs who talked down to their students.

Life was much more interesting out of school. Maya and Bailey met gamblers and liquor salesmen, both in the busy streets and in the well-furnished living room of their large home. Over the years, Grandmother Baxter had become a precinct captain, a political position giving her enormous privileges and power within the community, including influence with the local police department.

After spending six months at Grandmother Baxter's house, the children moved in with Mother, who was working part-time as a card dealer in a gambling parlor. Mother's boyfriend, a somewhat older man called

Mr. Freeman, also lived with them. He was a foreman in the Southern Pacific railway yards.

Mother's house was big and elegant. Maya and Bailey each had a room of their own, ample food, and clothes bought in a store. They each had a radio and enough spending money to buy paperback books. Maya was given dancing lessons, and when Mother entertained, Maya was often asked to dance for guests. This was considered part of general hospitality at the time, and any guest with a special talent—singing, dancing, or reciting poetry—might also be asked to entertain.

In general, the children were well behaved and did as they were told, but Maya and Bailey sensed an implied threat that if either child truly upset Mother, they would be sent back to Stamps. This implied threat affected each child differently. Bailey began stuttering. Maya had terrible nightmares. Sometimes they got so bad that she was allowed to sleep with Mother and Mr. Freeman.

On one of these occasions, Mother left the house early the next morning. When Maya awoke a little later, Mr. Freeman, who was awake but still in bed, molested her. Maya didn't know whether his touching her private parts was bad or something that every father did once in a while.

When the incident had ended, Mr. Freeman asked Maya if she loved Bailey. "Yes," she said. Then he told her, "If you ever tell anybody what we did, I'll have to kill Bailey." Maya didn't understand what they had done or what there was to tell, but she certainly wasn't going to let anybody kill Bailey. So she kept the secret from both her mother and brother. It was the first secret she had ever kept from Bailey.

In an attempt to push the incident to the back of her mind, Maya began reading more and more. She got her first library card and then spent most Saturdays there. She especially loved stories like those written by Horatio Alger. In these stories, the poor main character always became rich—by hard work and honesty —and then did lots of good deeds. In general, Maya was a happy child at this point in her life.

Several months later, however, everything in her life changed. While Mother and Bailey were away from the house, Mr. Freeman grabbed eight-year-old Maya and raped her. He threatened to kill her if she screamed—and to kill Bailey if she told anyone. Terrified, she promised not to tell. But Mr. Freeman had seriously injured Maya. Later in the afternoon, she went to bed, hiding her bloodstained panties under the mattress. Maya thought she had done something wrong, and the pain was her punishment.

When Mother returned and found Maya in bed, she assumed that Maya was coming down with the measles. Mother left the room and told Bailey to get some cold towels to pat Maya's face. When Bailey left, Mr. Freeman walked into the room. "If you tell . . . ," he threatened.

In more than a hundred books, Horatio Alger—shown here in a painting by Steven Donahos—wrote about boys who rose from poverty to wealth through hard work and virtuous living.

In the morning, Mr. Freeman moved out. By then, Maya was delirious with a high fever. She sometimes called out to Bailey, asking him if they could run away. Other times she said she was dying, or that she wanted to die. Her bed sheets were soaked with sweat. Mother wanted to put on clean sheets, but to do so, she had to move her daughter. Maya fought in terror whenever anyone touched her. Finally, while Mother cradled Maya in her arms, Bailey began changing the sheets. As he did this, the blood-soaked panties fell from under the mattress to Mother's feet.

Mother took Maya to the hospital, where Bailey insisted she must tell about what happened or the man would hurt another little girl. Maya kept repeating that Mr. Freeman would kill Bailey if she said anything. But Bailey convinced her this wasn't true, so Maya told him all about the rape. Bailey started to cry, then Maya cried too. Bailey then told Grandmother Baxter, and Mr. Freeman was arrested.

The day of the trial, the courtroom was filled with spectators. Mr. Freeman's attorney cross-examined the terrified eight-year-old. Among other questions, the attorney asked Maya if Mr. Freeman had ever touched her body before the alleged rape. Maya was afraid to say "yes," imagining that people would be angry with her and stone her for being a wanton woman, like they did in the Bible. And Mother, who believed Maya was a good girl, would be disappointed in her. Plus she had kept a secret from Bailey, which she had never done before. Everyone would get mad at her. So Maya lied and said that Mr. Freeman had never touched her before. She felt the lie was going to choke her right there on the witness stand. Maya had to be carried off the stand because she was so frightened that she could no longer walk.

Mr. Freeman was sentenced to one year and one day in jail, but his attorney got him out that same day. Several hours later, a policeman rang the doorbell of Grandmother Baxter's home. Still terrified, Maya thought the policeman had come to get her, having found out about her lie on the witness stand. But the policeman told the family that Mr. Freeman had apparently been kicked to death, then dumped behind the local slaughterhouse. The person or persons who killed him were never identified. At the time, however, some people believed Maya's uncles had taken their revenge.

But Maya was certain that Mr. Freeman died because she lied on the witness stand, saying Mr. Freeman hadn't molested her before the rape. She thought her lying voice had killed him. She decided that if she spoke, her evil voice might just go out on its own and kill innocent people. She stopped speaking so nobody else would die. The only person she would talk to was Bailey.

Without speech, Maya learned to listen to everything. "I could just go into a room and I could just absorb sound . . . ," she recalled later. Initially the family attributed this to shock resulting from the rape. But after a few weeks, surely the child had healed? So the family thought Maya was being both sassy and sullen. Every so often, she was spanked for not answering when spoken to.

Three months passed. The family didn't know how to deal with the eight-year-old's completely silent, sad behavior. So Maya and Bailey were placed on a train to Stamps, Arkansas, to once again live with their grandmother, "Momma" Annie Henderson. They had spent a total of eight months with their mother in St. Louis. Bailey cried, wanting to stay in St. Louis. But

Maya, who not so long ago had dreaded being sent back to Stamps, now looked forward to once again living in the quiet, desolate, little town.

Maya did not speak in public for years. But she listened intently, turning her entire body into an "ear," remembering every inflection, every nuance of the words she heard. Many people in the Quarters thought Maya was retarded and openly talked about her as if she didn't understand. But Momma Annie never got discouraged by Maya's silence. It wasn't important to her that Maya talk, because Momma believed that when her granddaughter and the good Lord were ready, Maya was going to "become a preacher." For Maya, life passed by as if she were in a thick gray fog.

James Weldon Johnson was one of Maya's favorite writers. In 1900 he wrote the lyrics for the song "Lift Every Voice and Sing," sometimes called the black American national anthem.

Chapter FIVE

FOR LOVE OF POETRY

WHEN MAYA WAS 10 YEARS OLD, SHE MET Bertha Flowers, the wealthiest black woman in Stamps. The elegantly dressed Mrs. Flowers often made purchases at the Store, each time taking notice of the silent little girl. Usually Bailey carried Mrs. Flowers's packages home, but one afternoon, she asked that "Marguerite" do it.

Momma hurriedly changed Maya's clothes. Carrying the purchases, Maya followed Mrs. Flowers home. As they walked, Mrs. Flowers mentioned she had heard Marguerite did good written work at school, read a lot at school and home, but wouldn't speak in class.

Maya kept silent. Mrs. Flowers kept talking. She asserted that no one would force Marguerite to talk, but since Marguerite loved the written word, she should realize the human voice gave special life to words in books. Therefore, when they got to her house, she was going to lend Marguerite some books, which Marguerite was to read aloud. Marguerite should also say each sentence several different ways to discern how the human voice and its inflections could change a word's meaning.

Arriving at Mrs. Flowers's home, they sat down in the kitchen. Mrs. Flowers began reading aloud. Her voice was serene, well educated, and beautiful. "It was the best of times and the worst of times...," she said, holding a small book written by Charles Dickens.

Paul Laurence Dunbar was one of the most popular American poets of the 1890s and early 1900s. He was the first black American to become nationally popular as a writer of both poetry and fiction.

Langston Hughes published works in all forms of literature, but he was best known for his poetry and his sketches about an uneducated but proud and outspoken black man called "Simple."

A Tale of Two Cities was already one of Maya's favorite books, but hearing it spoken was even more wonderful. It sounded just as lovely as her favorite church music. Suddenly, for the first time in two years, Maya began to feel happy.

Mrs. Flowers gave her a book of poems. She instructed Maya to memorize one of the poems and be able to recite this on her next visit. Poetry is music written for the human voice, Mrs. Flowers said. A person who truly loves poetry reads it aloud.

A new world had suddenly opened up, and Maya eventually read every book in her school's small library. She didn't understand all of them, but she read them anyway because they made her feel special. In between library visits, Mrs. Flowers brought her more

W.E.B. Du Bois was the first black person to receive a Ph.D. degree at Harvard University. During the first half of the 1900s, he became the leading black opponent of racial discrimination.

books. Maya's favorite authors included black poet Paul Laurence Dunbar, black novelist and poet Langston Hughes, black poet James Weldon Johnson, and William Edward Burghardt (W.E.B.) Du Bois, economics professor and author of many books on the lives of black people. She enjoyed reading William Shakespeare's plays, initially believing him to be black because he used such wonderful language. In the very religious black Stamps community, Maya also read the Bible. Momma Annie commented that she loved to see Maya reading, especially poetry, because it "will put starch in your backbone."

Maya never really thought about how books actually got written, that they were done by a person with pen, pencil, paper. Occasionally she thought perhaps God and a writer got together, with the book coming out of some special writer's body part that only writers had. Eventually, she began writing poetry herself. After finishing a piece, Maya would retreat to a special quiet corner of the Store and read it aloud, enjoying the feel of the words. Customers in the Store began remarking that Annie Henderson's granddaughter seemed to be always reading aloud and writing, and sometimes they had to rap loudly on the counter to get her attention when they needed help.

Constantly encouraged by Momma and Uncle Willie, Maya also wrote regularly in a journal. It was her way of keeping in touch with the world around her, since she still refused to converse with anybody in public. Even at school, when other students gave oral reports, Maya would get her grade improved through better writing. She worked on her math with Uncle Willie at the Store. He would consistently instruct her, "do your sevensies, do your ninesies."

By the time she was 11, Maya's life had assumed a comfortable routine, including regular chores, and a weekly 10¢ allowance, which she gave to Bailey to buy cowboy books for her to read. The family had fish fries, went blackberry picking, and held picnics. Maya played games, such as hopscotch and jacks. Slowly she began to talk in public, at first with only family and a few special friends. By the time she was in the eighth grade, Maya talked as if she had never stopped talking. She became known throughout the black community as a precocious and eloquent child.

Although her own life seemed comfortable, Maya noticed the cotton pickers who came to the Store after work, the women's feet swollen, the men with torn overalls and shirts. She wondered how a just and fair God could let all this happen.

Sometimes the children had to run errands for Momma in the whitefolks' section of Stamps. The segregation was so complete that most black children weren't certain what whitefolks actually looked like. Because of Ku Klux Klan actions in the area, black children developed a thorough fear of these unknown "pale creatures" with their "see-throughy" skin, who

Members of the Ku Klux Klan confronting a group of young people in 1938

Joe Louis held the world heavyweight boxing title from 1937 to 1949—a longer reign than any other champion in the history of professional boxing.

sometimes injured or killed a black person for no reason other than skin color.

In a world where black people were devalued outside their own community, any black person who became famous to any degree was a national black hero. Boxing was one of the very few integrated sports in the United States, and Joe Louis, "The Brown Bomber," was a champion of black spirit.

In June 1936, Louis, until then undefeated, had been knocked out in 12 rounds by Germany's Max Schmeling. This was a propaganda victory for Hitler. When

Louis lost to Schmeling, the Nazi weekly journal wrote "It was a question of prestige for our race."

However, in June 1938 there was a rematch with Schmeling. In Momma's store, people kept wedging themselves into every available space, listening to the radio. The match was called the "USA versus the Nazis." The Brown Bomber humiliated Schmeling by knocking him out in the first round. Maya could not contain her excitement. Identifying with Louis, she felt that she was a part of the strongest people in the world.

In 1940, 12-year-old Maya graduated with honors from the eighth grade at Lafayette Country Training School for blacks—two buildings set on a dirt hill, unlike the white Central School, which had both a lawn and a tennis court. She was at the head of her class, with no absences, no tardies.

While only a small proportion of the class would be going on to agricultural and mechanical (A&M) schools, which trained black youth to be farmers, maids, handymen, carpenters, and baby nurses, there was still a future to look forward to. At graduation, all the children were dressed in their very best clothes, including new shoes for those who could afford them. Some children and adults even had ready-made clothes from the Sears or Wards catalogue. Proudly sitting with the other graduates, Maya hoped the sunlit memory of that morning would never end.

Everybody sang the American national anthem and recited the Pledge of Allegiance. The principal gave a short welcoming speech, and the Baptist minister led them in prayer. Then the principal gave a longer speech, talking about Booker T. Washington, who had been born a slave. Washington had gone on to found and become head of Tuskegee Institute. He was a highly esteemed author on racial and educational subjects. The principal's speech was truly inspiring.

Then came an invited guest speaker, a white politician running for reelection. This man spoke proudly of how the white children graduating from Central School would go on to become famous scientists, inventors and artists. He followed this by talking about how black students might aspire to become sports heroes. So, the politician promised, if he won re-election, he would see that the town of Stamps would get "the only colored paved playing field in that part of Arkansas."

Maya was furious. Why did they have to sit there quietly and be insulted for no reason other than the color of their skin? The children, who moments earlier had been proud and excited, hung their heads. They had once again been reminded that they were "Negro" and therefore had no control over their lives and achievements. As Maya marched up to get her diploma, she felt angry and almost defeated.

Her classmate Henry Reed delivered the valedictory address, "To Be or Not to Be," based on the theme from Shakespeare's play *Hamlet*. Then Reed paused. Something was about to happen. Maya could just feel

Booker T. Washington was an American educator and the founder of Tuskegee Institute.

it. Reed turned away from the audience and toward the graduates. Then he began singing—almost reciting—"Lift Every Voice and Sing," which was generally considered to be the black American national anthem. The poem, written by James Weldon Johnson, had been set to music by J. Rosamond Johnson. The poem was about the stony road that must be traveled by weary feet until they come to the place their parents had longed for. Soon everybody in the audience was singing along with Reed, including Maya. When the singing concluded, several people were crying. Maya lifted up her head. She was once more a proud member of the "wonderful, beautiful, Negro race."

Overt racism continued to affect her early life, however. For example, white doctors and dentists did not treat black patients. Black patients had to find black doctors and dentists, but there was no black dentist or doctor in Stamps.

When Maya developed an extremely painful toothache, Momma took her—with a white towel tied over her head and under her chin—to a white dentist in town. Momma had done business with the man over the years, but instead of being friendly, the dentist became very insulting. He wasn't going to treat a black person, not even a black child in pain. Maya and Momma had to travel by Greyhound bus to get Maya's tooth taken care of by a black dentist in Texarkana, 25 miles away.

Nor were blacks allowed in white hotels. So, when traveling, they often stopped at black churches, asking the ministers or deacons for help in finding a place to sleep for the night. Church officials would select a home and escort the strangers to it. Word traveled quickly in the community, and soon people were knocking quietly at a host's back door, bringing food for the strangers. Maya enjoyed meeting the many visitors who stayed at Momma's home.

Maya attended George Washington High School, which was located in a white residential district of San Francisco.

Chapter **SIX**

SAN FRANCISCO

A FEW MONTHS AFTER GRADUATION, MOMMA TOLD the children that they were going to California to live with their parents. Mother had moved to Oakland, a town near San Francisco, and Father lived in Los Angeles. Maya suspected the change was to get her and Bailey out of the sometimes dangerous South. California didn't have Ku Klux Klan lynch parties, and a black child could aspire to become something other than a farmer or a cleaning woman.

Initially Maya and Bailey stayed in Los Angeles. Then Mother drove the two children to Oakland, where they lived with her and Grandmother Baxter in a small apartment so near the railroad tracks that it shook every time a Southern Pacific train went by.

Mother soon married Daddy Clidell, a successful businessman, and the family moved to a 14-room house in San Francisco's Fillmore District. A succession of roomers—with varied accents and personalities—came to the home. At one time, the area had been predominantly inhabited by Japanese people, but by the beginning of World War II, Fillmore residents were mostly black. The Japanese had been removed to internment camps because the United States was at war with Japan. Black people were eagerly sought to fill war-related jobs in the shipyards and ammunition plants. Blacks came to the cities from the poor farmlands of the South in large numbers. Perhaps for the first time in the United States, blacks were able to think of themselves as important and appreciated.

The Fillmore District was a whirlwind of ongoing activity. Maya loved living in San Francisco and considered herself part of the city and of the exciting times surrounding it. There were weekly air-raid warnings, civil defense drills at school, and groups of young sailors wandering the streets. For Maya and Bailey, San Francisco was not only beautiful, it was freedom.

Maya had her 13th birthday. By now she was very self-conscious about her height, over five feet nine inches. Not only was she taller than most of the people her age, she was still growing. And it didn't help at all when people living in their boarding house kept asking her to reach for high-up things or to help them move things. She "felt like a horse."

At first, Maya attended a local high school for girls, but she was unhappy there. She had been advanced two semesters due to her good grades and excellent reading and math skills, but the school had students from varied ethnic groups, each with its own prejudices. Maya transferred to George Washington High School in a white residential district. During her first semester, she was one of three black students there. Each weekday she rode the streetcar, passing from the black section to the white section with a sense of dread. On the way home, she had a wonderful sense of relief when she saw black faces just like hers walking down the street.

But she was not the high achiever at this high school that she had been at her previous schools. Other students, with stronger educational backgrounds, surrounded her. These students spoke up quickly and confidently when a teacher asked a question. Unlike them, Maya felt she had to be absolutely certain of her facts before calling attention to herself. Sometimes she felt left out. But that was before she met Miss Kirwin, the civics and current events teacher. Miss Kirwin attempted to bring out the best in each student. She was always polite and encouraging to everybody, regardless of race or ethnic group. She made a tremendous impression on Maya's thinking about equality and opportunity.

When Maya was 14, she received a scholarship to take some classes in drama and dance at the California

Duke Ellington watches dancing couples from the stage. He was an American jazz bandleader, composer, and pianist, and he rates as one of the greatest figures in jazz.

Labor School, a college for adults. At first she was very shy in dance class, since she thought her body was "cucumber-shaped," with knobs for knees, elbows, and breasts. Locally, however, she began performing for the Elks and Eastern Star service organizations, and when she had free time, Maya started writing songs.

Daddy Clidell liked to play cards. At home, he taught Maya to play poker, jick, blackjack, and tonk. He became the father that Maya had never truly had. He introduced her to the black underground and to successful con men, who taught her how to avoid becoming a "mark," or target, for crooks.

When Maya was 15, Daddy Bailey invited her to spend the summer in southern California. Bailey Sr. worked in the kitchen of a naval hospital. He was also a Mason, an Elk, and the first Negro deacon in the Lutheran church. And he spoke fluent Spanish and encouraged Maya to learn the language. Maya and her father even visited Mexico together, since Bailey Sr.

had many acquaintances there.

Maya did not get along with her father's girlfriend, Delores, and the dislike seemed mutual. When Delores called Maya's mother a "whore," they got into a violent argument, and Maya ended up running away. She packed sandwiches, put three dollars in her pocket, and spent the day wandering the streets of Los Angeles and reading in the library.

As night fell, Maya began searching for a safe place to spend the night. She found an old gray car in a junkyard and decided to sleep in it. As usual, she said her prayers before falling asleep.

In the morning, Maya awoke to a ring of faces around the car windows. The faces were those of homeless teens who made the junkyard their home. Maya explained she had no place to go, and she stayed with the group for almost a month. Finally she telephoned Mother, asking to go home. Mother sent a plane ticket, and Maya returned to San Francisco.

Back in San Francisco, Maya and Bailey began attending the big-band dances in the city's large public auditorium. They danced the jitterbug, the Big Apple, the Lindy, and the Halftime Texas Hop, to the music of Duke Ellington, Count Basie, and Cab Calloway. But 16-year-old Bailey was increasingly adopting a wilder lifestyle. Mother and he fought about this, and finally Mother told him to leave her home. As he packed, he gave Maya his precious books. She couldn't stop crying. Bailey was her best friend in the world.

Maya became the first black person to work on the San Francisco streetcars. The famous cable cars add charm to the beautiful city.

Chapter **SEVEN**

MAYA BECOMES A MOTHER

AFTER HER TRIP TO MEXICO, HER MONTH IN THE junkyard, and Bailey's departure, Maya's exciting life in San Francisco suddenly seemed empty. She longed for some sort of change in her life. After much thought, she decided to get a job as a streetcar conductor. Before the war, all the streetcar workers had been male. But with men away in the service, women had taken over many of their former jobs, including streetcar service. A recent *San Francisco Chronicle* newspaper advertisement sought streetcar workers.

Maya decided it would be splendid to wear a blue suit and go up and down the hilly San Francisco streets with a money changer on her conductor's leather belt. Mother informed her that "colored people" were not hired to work the streetcars. But Mother had also told Maya there was nothing she couldn't do if she really tried.

Maya returned to the Market Street Railway Company office many times. Each time she was turned away with one excuse or another. She stubbornly persisted until one day the receptionist handed her a job application to fill out. Maya was only 15, but she quickly transformed herself into a 19-year-old on paper. Her prior job experience, she wrote, was as a companion and driver for a white lady, Mrs. Annie Henderson, in Stamps, Arkansas.

Maya became the first black person to work on the San Francisco streetcars. By the time the new school semester started, she had her own bank account, new clothes that she had purchased herself, and a new self-image. But she had also participated in such an entirely different world than her more sheltered classmates that she didn't seem to fit in with the other students at school anymore. By the time she was 16, formal schooling had become boring, and Maya began cutting classes—sometimes just to walk in Golden Gate Park, the city's chief recreational area.

Maya decided she needed a boyfriend. Since no prospects were in view, Maya decided to take charge of the situation herself. She selected one of the handsomest young men in the neighborhood and forthrightly invited him to have sex with her. The young man was quite surprised—but certainly willing. They went to a furnished room occupied by a friend and had intercourse—briefly and unemotionally. Afterward, they went their separate ways. Maya gave the act and the beau no more thought until three weeks later, when she discovered she was pregnant.

Initially she confided in her brother Bailey, who advised her not to tell their mother. Mother might make Maya quit high school before she got her diploma. So Maya hid her pregnancy under large clothes and pretended there was nothing unusual about her life. Mother, who was busy with business and her own life, never noticed.

In 1945, 16-year-old Maya graduated from Mission High School. That same evening she left a note on her stepfather's bed stating that she was expecting a baby and she was sorry for disgracing her family. Mother wanted to know who the baby's father was. Maya told her. Did Maya want to marry this young man? No. Did he want to marry her? No. That was the end of the questioning. Three weeks later, Clyde Bailey Johnson was born.

World War II ended in 1945, but it had changed society. Minorities and women of all races had learned new skills and life alternatives while working in the war industries. After the war, these industries shut down or converted to produce different merchandise, and the white males returning from the war wanted their former jobs back. Black people, like other minorities and white women, often found themselves unemployed again. The economy, which had boomed while producing war supplies, began to slow down.

Many of the paying boarders in Mother's big house began looking for work in more industrialized areas, such as Chicago, Detroit, and Los Angeles. Maya decided to move out too. She wanted to show the world—and her parents—that she could take care of herself and her much loved baby, Clyde.

Maya applied for a job as telephone operator with the local telephone company. She was turned down for reasons that she attributed to prejudice. She was told that she had failed a very basic IQ test. The telephone company could, however, give her a job clearing tables in its cafeteria. Maya took the job but quit just one week later.

While looking for work again, she passed a local Creole restaurant with a sign that said COOK WANTED. The pay was good, so Maya told the owner that she knew a great deal about cooking Creole style—a mixture of Spanish, French, and black cuisine. Maya also said she was 19, rather than 17. The owner saw no reason to question this since Maya was almost six feet tall and looked mature. She was also very polite and respectful. The owner particularly liked those characteristics, so he gave her the job. Maya asked one of Mother's tenants if he would please teach her to cook Creole. She learned quickly and quite enjoyed creating recipes and cooking food to perfection.

Maya rented a room for herself and Clyde in a Victorian mansion. She also fell in love with one of her customers, who eventually left her to marry his prior girlfriend. Maya became depressed. She had this dream of a considerate, hard-working husband, a little rose-covered cottage, and the ability to stay home and be a full-time mother. None of this was happening. Maya began to think life would never get better.

When she was 18, Maya decided she needed a change in scenery and traveled with her son to Los Angeles. There, Maya found a baby-sitter and rented a room in the baby-sitter's home. Then she got a job serving drinks at the Hi Hat Club, a nightclub, where her ability to remember drink orders got her good tips. Life began to look rosier. Her work shift began at 6:00 P.M. and ended at 2:00 A.M., so Maya had time to enjoy Clyde, telling him stories and reciting poems.

After a few months, she met two female customers who frequented the nightclub, and they invited her to their home for Sunday dinner. During the visit, they tried to introduce Maya to a lesbian lifestyle, but this didn't interest Maya. The women also discussed how they earned a limited income by sleeping with assorted clients. Eventually the discussion turned to the women's landlord, who wanted them to move because of their prostitution business. Pretending to be much more sophisticated than she actually was, Maya said she would rent the house in her name. The women could stay there, and Maya would help them find additional clients. In exchange, she would take a percentage of what they earned. To her surprise, the two women agreed to the proposition. At the age of 18, Maya had suddenly become the madam of "two whores and a whorehouse." She never saw the clients. She just came each evening to pick up her share of the money while continuing her work at the nightclub. She soon had saved enough money to buy a new, pale green Chrysler car, paying cash.

Life had become thoroughly enjoyable and affordable. Then, without warning, Maya got into an argument with the two prostitutes who worked for her. They threatened to tell the police about her activities as their employer. She became terrified that the police might decide she was an unfit mother and take Clyde away from her. Maya went home and packed her bags. The next morning, she and Clyde boarded a train to see Momma in Stamps, Arkansas, where Maya would feel safe. She had abandoned her new car in the railroad's parking lot because she was afraid the police would trace her through it.

Although Momma and Uncle Willie seemed the same, the war had changed Stamps, making it "swollen-belly poor." Most of the able-bodied young people, both black and white, had left during the war to find better-paying defense jobs in the North. When the war ended, few people returned to Stamps, where even low-paying jobs were scarce. The population of Stamps, both black and white, consisted mostly of elderly people and children.

At first Maya cried, but she discovered the Store hadn't changed. Shelves still had chewing tobacco and sardines, and Momma still had the wood-burning stove. As Clyde cuddled in Momma's arms, Maya began to adjust. To the black people of Stamps, however, she was a celebrity. Just about everybody stopped by, asking her to describe the many wonders of San Francisco. People liked to think a place existed where blacks were given opportunity and whites were not domineering and cruel.

Although Maya gradually became accustomed to the slower-paced community, she did not adjust well to the open racial bias which marked Southern life. She had lived relatively free of that treatment in San Francisco, and she saw no reason to accept it in Stamps. She began asserting herself, but one day, while shopping in the white section of town, she spoke back briskly to a rude white salesclerk. Momma got the news quickly and was waiting for Maya's return. Life in Stamps had become too dangerous for Maya and Clyde. Momma and Willie would also be in danger if Maya stayed. Momma had been warned that the Ku Klux Klan might come calling.

Maya with a portrait of Clyde as a young boy

Chapter **EIGHT**

TROUBLED TIMES

LESS THAN A YEAR AFTER MOVING TO STAMPS, Maya returned to San Francisco. She moved into Mother's new 14-room house. Her brother, Bailey, was also living there. The walls were covered with Mother's diplomas in cosmetology, barbering, and welding. Mother's energy had not diminished, but Bailey's seemed to have changed directions. He used to be outgoing, but he had become quiet and had lost the spark in his dark eyes. He had little time for Maya and Clyde. He always seemed to be busy with something, but Maya couldn't figure out what that was. She worried that her much loved brother would end up like so many discouraged local young people, hooked on cocaine, heroin, or some other deadly drug.

Maya found a job as a short-order cook at a small restaurant. She became friendly with the owner of a record store across the street and began collecting blues and jazz. At the same time, Maya thought about finding a career for herself, a profession with a future. But jobs for women were not plentiful, and secretarial work demanded good shorthand and typing skills, which she didn't have.

Posters encouraged young people to join the army. Maya thought that if she signed up for two years and saved her pay, she could buy a house when she got out. She might even get professional training so she could get a good job. Mother agreed to find child care for Clyde. She also suggested that Maya apply for Officer Candidate School rather than just enlisting in the Women's Army Corps (WAC). That made possibilities even brighter in Maya's eyes.

She filled out the official forms. Since the army didn't accept women with children, Maya checked the "no children" blank on the application. She easily passed the Officer Candidate School intelligence test. She also passed the physical exam, despite her worries about prior childbirth being discovered. She was accepted for Officer Candidate School and told that she would leave for training in just a few months. Maya gave away most of her books and donated her clothes to charity. She quit her temporary short-order cook job to spend more time with Clyde before she left.

Then someone from the army recruitment center

called and ordered Maya to get over there right away. Maya hurried over, assuming someone had found out about Clyde, but that wasn't the problem. An officer told Maya that records showed she had attended the California Labor School—where she had studied dance and drama—and the House Un-American Activities Committee listed the school as a Communist organization. No Communists were permitted in the military. Even though Maya had never been a member of the Communist Party, she was abruptly dismissed for having attended the school.

Maya found herself without a job and with few clothes. Once again, she began thinking that she would never accomplish anything in life. She accepted a job as a night-shift waitress in a small restaurant called the Chicken Shack. One day a young man, R. L. Poole, rang the doorbell at Mother's house. He was looking for a female dancer to accompany his tap-dancing act, and the woman at the record shop had given him Maya's name and address, since she had frequently talked about dance. The army had punished her for studying at the California Labor School, but Mr. Poole might reward her efforts. Maya had also won dance contests in the past and knew the current dances. She didn't have any professional experience, but she auditioned anyhow and got the job.

At her first public appearance, Maya wore a red, white, and blue costume that looked like a one-piece bathing suit, and she carried a cane. During her first appearance in front of an audience, she experienced stage fright and could barely move. But after that, she enjoyed the applause.

In the meantime, Bailey had fallen in love with and married Eunice, a former classmate who seemed to have straightened out his life. Mother helped Maya devise dance routines. Maya hoped the situation would continue forever and keep getting better, but it didn't. R. L. announced abruptly that he was teaming up once again with his former dance partner and girl-friend. Maya's job hunting began once again.

One of Mother's friends in Stockton, California, needed a fry cook for her restaurant. Maya moved there with her son and hired a baby-sitter called Big Mary. Maya continued to daydream about a good man who would love her and her son and be a good provider. They would live together forever in a pretty little house. She would have two children, a boy and a girl, and would not have to work but could stay home and cook.

One day, when Maya was about 20, she met an older man, called L. D. Tolbrook, at the restaurant. He was about twice her age and appeared to be wealthy and attracted to Maya. They soon began dating, then be-came lovers. Sometimes L.D. took Maya to visit vari-ous buildings, where he would briefly chat with the women residents and then leave. Maya realized these women were prostitutes, but she also naively believed that L.D. truly loved and wanted to marry her.

One evening, her usually confident boyfriend looked

quite tired and sad. He explained that he had lost a lot of money gambling. Since he couldn't pay the gambling debt, the other gamblers, members of a criminal mob, were going to come after him. He would have to leave town quickly.

Maya didn't want him to go, because she hoped to marry him someday. At his prompting, Maya even agreed to become a prostitute—to sell her body—and give L.D. the money she earned so he could pay his gambling debts. When L.D. came to pick her up after her first week at work, he complained that she hadn't made enough money and urged her to try harder.

When Maya picked up Clyde one day after work, she received an emergency message from her family in San Francisco. Mother was in the hospital. Maya returned Clyde to Big Mary and boarded a bus to San Francisco. She went to the hospital to visit her mother, who was recovering from surgery, and learned that Bailey's wife, who had tuberculosis, also had pneumonia. Maya and Bailey sat in the hospital waiting room and cried together. Mother recovered, but Eunice died, and Bailey became inconsolable. He quit his job, behaved strangely, and looked unwell. When Maya tried to help him, he became angry.

During one of their arguments, Maya mentioned working as a prostitute to help L.D. pay his gambling debts. For a moment, Bailey was silent. Then he got angry and told Maya to get her son and return to San Francisco. If her boyfriend objected to this, Bailey said he would give the man more things to worry about than just gamblers.

Maya went back to Stockton, but when she arrived at Big Mary's home, it was boarded up and silent. She asked a neighbor where Big Mary had gone and learned that the baby-sitter had moved three days earlier. The other mothers who used Mary's services had been notified of the move and had picked up their children. Big Mary had proclaimed that Clyde had been given to her, and that she would take him with her wherever she went.

Maya panicked and went to L.D.'s house to see if he would help her find Clyde. His attractive wife answered the door. When L.D. came to the door, instead of offering help, he became angry with Maya for bothering him while he was at home with his family. He told her he would visit her if and when he found the time. Maya suddenly realized how stupid she had been. She later wrote that "stupidity had led me into a trap where I had lost my baby."

After leaving L.D.'s house, Maya remembered that Big Mary had said something about having a brother in Bakersfield. She went there the next day, asking all over town about Big Mary's brother. Finally, she was directed to a farm on the outskirts of town. When she got there, she saw Clyde playing in the mud. Big Mary begged to keep the boy, but Maya refused. With Clyde in her arms, she fled back to San Francisco, where they again moved in with her mother.

Once again, Maya began looking for work. Finally, she got a job planning menus for a restaurant in Oakland. The owner of the restaurant was also in the prizefighting business. He was training several prizefighters, and part of Maya's job involved driving them around. This seemed quite exciting, until Maya actually watched a prize fight. She witnessed one of her fighter friends getting hurt in the ring, so Maya stood up and tried to stop the fight. She was quickly fired.

Then one day she met Troubadour Martin, a man who had frequented the restaurant, and he offered her a job running a fitting room in her home for women clients who bought clothes from him. Maya guessed the clothes were probably stolen, but at least the job would let her spend more time at home with her son.

As the weeks passed, Maya began to think that she was in love with Martin, but he was indifferent to her attentions, and his thoughts always seemed to be somewhere else. When Maya persisted with the relationship, Martin said he had something to show her. He drove her to a horrible waterfront slum. Entering the building, she saw addicts of all ethnic groups slumped around the room, half asleep.

To discourage her attentions, he made Maya watch as he injected heroin into his arm—one of the scariest things Maya had ever seen. Right then, she decided that criminal life was not for her. She decided that she was going to make something special of her life—even though she didn't know what that would be.

During the mid-1950s, Maya began a career as a singer and dancer—first at the Purple Onion, a San Francisco nightclub, and then as part of the chorus of Porgy and Bess, *a popular folk opera.*

Chapter **NINE**

PORGY AND BESS

MOTHER OFFERED HER MONEY, BUT **21**-YEAR-old Maya refused to take it. Instead, she began working at both a dress shop and a small real estate office. Her salary barely covered the cost of rent, food, and her 5-year-old son's baby-sitter. She purchased clothing at thrift shops, usually choosing something colorful. Maya loved color, headbands, and beads.

On days when she could find time, she went to Clyde's elementary school just to watch him. After several visits, Clyde suggested that she not go to the school unless her presence was requested. He also mentioned that if she did visit, it would be nice if she wore sweater sets. Maya didn't understand this request at first. Finally she realized Clyde wanted her to wear the matching pullover-cardigan sets that the white mothers wore.

Maya sometimes visited the Melrose Record Shop, located in San Francisco's Fillmore District. The shop was a gathering place for local musicians and record collectors. The owner of the store, Louise Cox, was a very friendly person. At first, Maya was suspicious about Louise because white women were seldom that congenial with her. One day, Louise offered Maya a job. At first, Maya hesitated, wondering what the woman wanted in return. But the salary that Cox offered was better than what she was getting at the dress shop and the real estate office, so Maya decided to accept the job offer and see what happened.

At the Melrose Record Shop, Maya met all kinds of musicians—both black and white—and a diverse clientele. She also met a white sailor, Tosh Angelos, who was of Greek origin. Tosh became a regular customer. When he left the navy, he began work in an electrical appliance store. He and Maya enjoyed long conversations. Tosh often told Maya that he liked chatting with her because she told the truth. They began dating regularly, and Tosh took a special interest in little Clyde.

One day, Tosh proposed marriage. It was the first time Maya had had a marriage proposal, and she accepted. Mother objected to her marrying a white man, but finally she and Bailey gave grudging approval. Maya Angelos quit her job at the record store and became a full-time housewife. Finally, it seemed she had what she had hoped for—except for one small glitch. Tosh insisted that Maya stop seeing her former friends, and he would not allow Clyde's friends to visit. They were not worthy, Tosh said. He even objected to Maya going to church. Maya didn't mind this behavior at first, since Tosh liked being alone.

Church had always been an integral part of Maya's life, however, and she missed attending services. Eventually she began attending in secret, going to a different church each time, so Tosh wouldn't find out. Maya made it a point not to become friendly with any of the other church attendees, but one day, she was so excited and uplifted by a service at the Evening Star Baptist Church that she signed up to become a member. A church member telephoned her that same week. Tosh was furious. Maya kept silent and tried to conform to her husband's way of thinking.

The marriage limped along until one day Tosh said that he was tired of being married. Although Maya realized their marriage was far from perfect, she hadn't expected it to end so suddenly. She had been faithful to Tosh and let him have his way most of the time. They hadn't even been married a full three years.

Although they continued living together for monetary reasons, Maya felt increasingly miserable. Then she needed some minor surgery, but due to complications, she had to stay in the hospital for several weeks. When she finally returned home, Maya told Tosh that she was going to Stamps, Arkansas, to visit her grandmother. She thought of Stamps as a safe and secure place—something she truly needed. At that point, Tosh told Maya that her beloved grandmother had died while Maya was in the hospital.

She and Tosh divorced, and Maya and Clyde moved back to her mother's house. Maya started job hunting again. She looked at many positions, but few jobs paid a decent salary. Then she saw a sign: FEMALE DANCERS WANTED—GOOD PAY. The place was a strip joint, where women danced only partially clothed in fancy costumes.

Using the name Rita, Maya auditioned and was hired. Although she was not expected to take off her clothes, she was expected to sell watered-down drinks and expensive champagne to the customers between shows. Although it certainly wasn't a good job, Maya thought that at least she was dancing. She ordered some fancy costumes and created her act.

Maya got along well with the customers. She even told them that they were buying watered-down drinks. They appreciated her honesty and bought the champagne—which cost more—instead. When the other women selling drinks noticed that Maya was making more money, they complained to the boss. Maya was given notice that her job was about to end.

One night, shortly before she was to leave, Maya observed three elegantly dressed men and a lovely woman who had been sitting in the audience. She learned that the woman worked as a singer at the Purple Onion, a famous San Francisco nightclub. This elite group began coming regularly to see Maya dance. One of the men mentioned that the female singer was leaving the Purple Onion, and he asked if Maya could sing.

Maya had sung in church services while growing up in Stamps, but not professionally. She auditioned anyway, and she was hired. She decided she needed a stage name. Her first name, Maya, would be fine, but she needed a new last name. After some experimentation with sounds, the Purple Onion management changed her last name—Angelos—and, at 26, she became Maya Angelou.

At the Purple Onion, Maya got professional lessons on stage dress and conduct. Initially she was terrified of appearing before a crowd of more than 200 people, but once she started to sing, all her worries disappeared. She was popular immediately, and as her reputation spread, she was invited to participate in radio talk-shows and to sing on television programs. Newspapers called for interviews, and a small Maya Angelou fan club even evolved.

One evening, friends told Maya that there was an opening in a Broadway musical for a singer. Maya wanted the job, but when she told the manager of the Purple Onion that she wanted to leave, he insisted that she could not break her contract. Maya thought she had lost her one big opportunity in show business.

A short time later, however, she noticed people that looked familiar in the Purple Onion audience. She finally remembered they were performers in *Porgy and Bess*, a popular folk opera about life among black people in Charleston, South Carolina, in the 1920s. That evening, Maya received an unexpected invitation to join the chorus of *Porgy and Bess*. This time, with some help, she managed to get out of her contract. Because the opera was being performed in theaters around the world, Maya had to leave Clyde once again—this time with her mother.

The cast and crew of *Porgy and Bess* eventually traveled to 22 countries. Maya was enjoying her new career until a letter arrived from Mother. Clyde was sick with some kind of strange rash that doctors seemed

In 1957, Maya appeared in a Columbia Pictures movie called Calypso Heat Wave.

unable to cure. Maya left the cast and returned home as quickly as she could. Clyde felt miserable and barely looked at her. Maya, feeling guilty, promised that she would never leave him again.

Maya was home, but life there had changed. Not only was she out of work, but Bailey was in prison for selling stolen goods. Seriously depressed, Maya telephoned a psychiatrist and asked him to see her on an emergency basis. At the last moment, however, she decided not to go. Could a middle-aged white man begin to understand her problems as a black mother, a black woman, and a black artist? She didn't think so.

Instead, Maya visited a musician friend. This person insisted she make a list of all the good things in her life: her son, wonderful mother, excellent hearing, keen vision, dancing success, etc. After looking at the list she constructed, Maya realized that she should be grateful for all the good things in her life, not sad about the bad things.

Maya began taking theater jobs that allowed her to spend as much time as possible with her son. With his mother home, Clyde slowly recovered from his mysterious illness and regained his usual spunk. For example, one day he walked into Maya's room to announce that he had changed his name. From that point on, his name was "Guy." Why? No particular reason. It was just that "Clyde" sounded mushy to him, and he was not going to change his mind about the matter. He didn't, and from that point forward, he was called Guy.

National Guardsmen turned away a young black woman as she attempted to enter Central High School in Little Rock, Arkansas, in 1957—a period of great racial unrest in the United States.

Chapter **TEN**

AFRICA

IN **1957,** AMERICANS BEGAN MAKING DRAMATIC changes in racial policies and personal lifestyles. Because of new laws, schools that had allowed only white students to attend were required to let black children enroll. Many people in the South protested the decision and refused to let black students enter. In Little Rock, Arkansas, Governor Orval Faubus called out the National Guard to block integration of a formerly all-white high school. When a court injunction removed the guardsmen, riots followed. At that point, President Dwight Eisenhower sent in federal troops to enforce integration.

At about the same time, beatnik culture became a popular lifestyle. At 29, Maya moved to a houseboat which was part of a commune in Sausalito, California, across the bay from San Francisco. For a while, Maya and Guy enjoyed the casual way of life in the commune, but in less than a year, group living lost its appeal. In 1958, Maya and Guy moved to Laurel Canyon, an attractive residential area near Hollywood that was almost all white. Initially, when Maya tried to rent a house, she was told that it had already been taken. She then asked two white friends to try to rent the house for her. They succeeded, and Maya moved in.

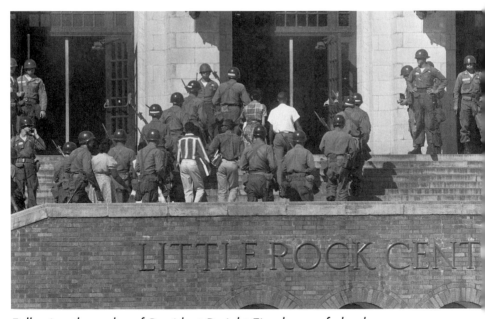

Following the order of President Dwight Eisenhower, federal troops escorted black students from their homes to their high school classes in Little Rock, Arkansas.

But racial bias was also evident at the local school, and it interfered with Guy's education. Maya and her son moved to the more ethnically diverse Westlake area of Los Angeles, where Mexican, Asian, black, and white families lived side by side. Maya began to write while living there. About a year and a half later, a literary friend urged her to move to New York and join the Harlem Writers' Guild, noted for encouraging the work of prominent and promising black writers, such as James Baldwin.

Maya considered the idea, but Mother's next project helped her decide. Mother had just joined the merchant marine as a member of the Marine Cooks and Stewards Union. Why would she want to do this, Maya wondered, considering all the other options Mother had. In response, Mother said she joined because someone had told her that the union didn't hire Negro women, that's why.

Maya moved to New York and made her first visit to the prestigious Harlem Writers' Guild. There, heart pounding, she read aloud her first adult piece, a play. Then she waited to hear what these famous literary people thought of her initial effort.

When Maya finished reading, one member promptly said the play was awful. Hearing this, Maya was ready to quit writing immediately. But another member told her not to be so sensitive. If she was going to be a writer, she would have to learn to accept criticism. If she couldn't do that, no one would give her worth-

Allen Ginsberg, poet laureate of the Beat Generation, addressed a group in Washington Square in New York City.

while suggestions. That advice made sense to Maya. She had been brought up knowing that to have talent was not enough—a person also had to work on improving that talent or skill. Much later in life, she would philosophize, "Not everything you do is going to be a masterpiece. . . . But you get out there and you really try and sometimes you really do, you write that masterpiece, you sing that classic."

Talented or not, writing wasn't paying the rent, so Maya once again began to sing at nightclubs—some good, some dingy. But then one day she went to hear the Reverend Martin Luther King Jr. speak at a Harlem church in which there was standing room only. King had just been released from jail for his civil rights work. He was touring the country to raise money for the Southern Christian Leadership Conference [SCLC] programs. The goal of this interracial, nonsectarian organization was to gain improved economic, civic, cultural, and religious rights through nonviolent action. Reverend King was the SCLC's first president. He had been born in segregated Atlanta, Georgia, and educated at Morehouse College, Crozer Theological Seminary, and Boston University, with special studies at Harvard and the University of Pennsylvania. King was considered by many to be one of the greatest leaders of the 20th century.

Maya, along with the rest of the church audience, was mesmerized by King's soul-stirring speech. She wanted to help him and his cause, so she began encouraging some of her theatrical friends to put on a show to raise funds for the SCLC. With the help of

Civil rights leader Martin Luther King Jr. speaking to a gathering in New York City

some friends, she found people to fund the show, a place to hold the show, a cast, and a crew. The show, "Cabaret for Freedom," was a huge success in 1960.

Sometime later, Maya was invited to a meeting at the Harlem office of the SCLC. Three administrators whom Maya had met while organizing "Cabaret for Freedom" offered her the position of SCLC coordinator. At first she was stunned by such an important job offer, but she decided to accept the position.

Both adults and children, white as well as black, volunteered time at the office and did whatever jobs needed to be done. Many white entertainers added their support to the civil rights struggle, and Maya discovered that the world of prejudice in which she had grown up was slowly beginning to change. Maya sent out SCLC information letters and fund-raising invitations by the tens of thousands, all in the name of Dr. King's movement. The mood of the nation was one of hope and action.

During this period, Maya met Thomas Allen, who worked as a bail bondsman. They dated for a while and then became engaged. The engagement abruptly ended when Maya met Vusumzi Make, a representative of the Pan African Congress in South Africa. Make was a member of the Xhosa tribe, a lawyer, and a South African freedom fighter in exile. At that time, South Africa was still governed under white rule.

Vusumzi's brilliant mind, his dedication to causes, and his charming British-Xhosa accent attracted

Maya, and the attraction was mutual. Two weeks after they met in 1961, he proposed. Two weeks after that, they flew to London, England, to attend a conference of African freedom fighters.

In London, Maya met several women married to prominent black diplomats and black freedom fighters. After the conference, Maya flew back to New York City to find a new apartment, and Vus flew to Egypt for more meetings. Maya found and redecorated the new apartment. She worked long and hard in her role as homemaker—cleaning, ironing, and cooking fancy meals. But she continued to participate in the Harlem Writers' Guild and helped organize the Cultural Association of Women of African Heritage.

When Maya was offered a role in *The Blacks*, an off-Broadway play by French playwright Jean Genet, Vus refused to let her appear onstage. He felt it wasn't proper for the wife of an African leader to give a public performance. Eventually he talked with a friend, studied the play, and then insisted that Maya act in it because of the play's important message. As Vus became more and more occupied with business appointments and meetings at the United Nations, Maya's theater role became increasingly important to her. It provided intellectual stimulation as well as a distraction from the unfamiliar lipstick stains and traces of perfume on Vus's clothing. Maya suspected that Vus was seeing other women—an accusation that Vus vehemently denied.

Maya played a role in The Blacks, *an off-Broadway play by French playwright Jean Genet.*

Adding to these family problems, Maya began to receive terrifying phone threats from nameless callers who told her Vus was going to die, or that he was dead, or that Guy had been seriously injured and was in the hospital. Vus explained to Maya that all these threats came from the South African police, because he was an African leader and freedom fighter. Maya and Vus changed their home phone number repeatedly.

In the midst of all this, Maya received an eviction notice. She hadn't realized that Vus, who had taken total charge of their financial affairs, hadn't paid the rent on their lovely apartment. Vus told her not to worry about the rent, since they were moving to Egypt.

Maya and Guy flew to San Francisco to visit Mother, while Vus went to Cairo, Egypt, to make living arrangements for his family. A few weeks later, Maya and Guy joined him in Cairo. The city was different from anything they had imagined. The air was filled

This 1972 street scene of Cairo, Egypt, shows Al-Azhar University, a major center for the study of Islam, the religion of Muslims. The university was founded in A.D. 970 and ranks among the world's oldest. At right is a Muslim mosque.

with spicy scents, and street vendors of every kind offered their wares. Taxis competed for space with camels and limousines, and modern skyscrapers contrasted with the ancient custom of women dressed from head to toe in heavy, black clothing.

In Cairo, Maya felt like a heroine in an exotic novel. Vus had filled their luxurious apartment with beautiful furniture, tapestries, and Oriental rugs. Maya met freedom fighters from all over Africa, and she and Vus entertained frequently. Then, one day her maid informed Maya that the bills weren't being paid—not even the rent. Maya told Vus that she was going to work. Vus objected, explaining that proper women didn't work in Egypt, and his status as a leader did not permit her to accept a job. He insisted that the needed money would eventually come in from various sources.

Despite his initial objections, Vus accompanied Maya to work on her first day of employment as an associate editor at a magazine called the *Arab Observer.* She was one of only two black Americans working in the news medium in the Middle East. Through her new job, Maya met writers from all over the world. Initially, she thought she would never learn enough about Africa's complicated affairs to be able to write intelligently about them. But she read every book, magazine, and essay available, and she continu-

In 1962, Maya moved from Cairo, Egypt, to Accra, Ghana, with her son, Guy. This photo was taken in 1965.

ally consulted Vus, who was an expert on tribes, politics, leaders, and everything else in Africa. She worked at the magazine for more than a year. To supplement her salary, Maya also wrote radio commentary for Radio Egypt.

By his time, her marriage to Vus was deteriorating. Although Maya still admired Vus's work, she could not tolerate his unfaithfulness. Finally, in 1962, Maya announced she would be leaving for West Africa. Seventeen-year-old Guy enrolled at the University of Ghana, considered to be the best institute of higher learning in Africa. Vus offered no objections to their departure and contacted friends of his in Accra, the capital of Ghana, so Maya and Guy would have a place to stay when they arrived.

Accra was a phenomenal sight. Maya wandered the open marketplace, where black women sold everything from American face cream to fried ripe plantain chips called *killi wills*. Many black women dressed traditionally and walked gracefully with large baskets balanced on their heads, while others wore Western-style clothes. Maya heard many languages being spoken, including Fanti, Ga, Twi, Akan, Ewe, Moshi-Dagomba, pidgin, and English.

While Guy joined some of their host's friends for a picnic, Maya sorted through Guy's clothes to see what he could take to the university and what he might still need. She had just finished her task when she got a telephone call. Guy had been in an auto accident and

Maya enjoyed shopping at the open market in Accra. This woman is carrying yams—a staple food in Ghana—to sell at the market.

was seriously injured. Maya rushed to the hospital and learned that Guy had a broken neck, arm, and leg, as well as internal injuries. Following emergency surgery, he was placed in a full body cast and had to remain in the hospital for a month.

Maya had to find a job much more quickly than she had anticipated. She had some connections, however, and was soon employed as an administrative assistant at the School of Music and Drama at the University of Ghana's Institute of African Studies. She was able to stay at the home of an instructor who was away on leave for six months.

After discharge from the hospital, Guy needed care, and he stayed with Maya for three months. Then, still wearing a neck brace, he moved into a university dormitory. Maya was going to be truly alone for the first time. As Guy brought his trunk to the door, he hugged her. "Maybe now," he said, "you'll have a chance to grow up."

Maya made new friends, and together they laughed, joked, discussed politics, and talked about how wonderful it was to be in Africa. She became so fluent in the Fanti language that she was once mistaken for a tribal native. As a gourmet cook, she thoroughly enjoyed the local foods, such as lamb curry with side dishes of fresh pineapple, tomatoes, papaya, and mangos.

Sometimes Maya daydreamed about how her ancestors might have been fishers or market traders in Africa. Her travels throughout Ghana eased her prior worries about American blacks having lost their African heritage after being sold into slavery. She discovered that many customs she had grown up with in Stamps, Arkansas, were similar to those in Ghana— including the custom of calling people uncle, cousin, and brother as terms of respect and endearment.

After about three years in Ghana, Maya, like most of the other expatriates, increasingly realized that the United States was her true home. Although she had not consciously come to Ghana to find her roots, she had encountered them frequently. Her people had survived despite everything.

Maya is shown here with her first autobiographical book,
I Know Why the Caged Bird Sings, *published by Random House
in 1970.*

Chapter **ELEVEN**

THE WRITING PATH

WHEN MAYA WAS **38,** SHE RETURNED TO California. Two years later, she wrote and narrated a 10-part KQED educational television series called *Blacks, Blues, Black,* which highlighted African traditions still current in American life. Then one day her good friend, novelist James Baldwin, invited her to a small party at the home of noted editorial cartoonist Jules Feiffer. The day after the party, Feiffer's wife called an editor friend at Random House, a large New York publisher, and suggested that Maya Angelou be persuaded to write a book about her fascinating life.

Maya told the Random House editor that she wasn't the least bit interested in writing a book. The editor kept telephoning, and Maya kept refusing. Finally, the editor said he could understand her refusal because the job probably would be too difficult for her. Hearing that challenge, Maya immediately decided to write the book.

I Know Why the Caged Bird Sings was published in 1970, when Maya was 42 years old. It covers Maya's life from the time she arrived in Stamps, Arkansas, at age three, until the birth of her son when she was sixteen. The book's title originated with a poem called "Sympathy," by Paul Laurence Dunbar. The poem talks about knowing why the caged bird still sings and beats its wings: although it is caged, it still *wants* to be free. The book's dedication reads, "To my son, Guy Johnson, and all the strong black birds of promise who defy the odds and gods and sing their songs." *I Know Why the Caged Bird Sings* was nominated for a National Book Award, and Maya became the first African-American woman to make the nonfiction bestseller lists. This first book also became required reading at many universities. The theme shows that people can survive with courage and dignity— even in a hostile environment.

A succession of honors and accomplishments followed the success of Maya's first book, including her appointment as Poet in Residence at the University of Kansas and her designation as a Yale University Fellow. Someone at Columbia Pictures movie studio invited Maya to Hollywood to ask her to write a movie script for Alex Haley's book, the *Autobiography of*

Maya with her son, Guy

Malcolm X. Maya was enjoying her success. Only the death of her father marred her happiness.

In 1971, her first volume of poetry, *Just Give Me a Cool Drink of Water 'fore I Diiie,* was published and nominated for a Pulitzer Prize. Maya then lectured for the first time at Wake Forest University in North Carolina, a private, predominantly white school, where she received the North Carolina Award for Literature. At the close of her lecture, the audience of 600 people was so excited and enthusiastic, they stood up while asking question after question. It seemed Maya had ignited a spark and opened them up to new thoughts and directions.

In 1972, she wrote *Georgia, Georgia,* becoming the first African-American woman to have an original screenplay produced.

In 1972, Maya met builder and writer-cartoonist Paul Du Feu at a literary party in London, England. Du Feu had been born in England, attended architectural school, then graduated from the London School of Economics. He had been briefly married to feminist activist Germaine Greer, author of *The Female Eunuch.* Maya and Paul almost immediately fell in love, and they were married at the multiracial Glide Community Church in San Francisco in 1973, when Maya was 45.

The couple lived first in Los Angeles, then in Sonoma, where Paul bought, rebuilt, and sold old houses. Maya indulged in her long-term passion, gourmet cooking, and collected more than 100 cookbooks. Her son, Guy, continued to bring happiness into her life, and she welcomed a grandson, Colin Ashanti Murphy-Johnson, into her life as well.

Maya also continued to write. It took her three years to complete *Gather Together in My Name,* which was published in 1974. The book is dedicated to Maya's "blood brother," Bailey Johnson, and to her "other real brothers who encouraged me to be bodacious enough to invent my own life daily: James Baldwin, Kwesi Brew, David Du Bois, Samuel Floyd, John O. Killens, Vagabond King, Leo Maitland, Vusumzi Make, Julian Mayfield, Max Roach." There is a special thanks to her friend, Professor Dolly McPherson, whose doctoral dissertation examined and credited Maya Angelou's contributions to American cultural history. *Gather Together in My Name* covers the time period from World War II until Maya rescued her kidnapped son.

By 1974, Maya had also become Distinguished Visiting Professor at Wake Forest University, Wichita State University, and California State University at Sacramento. That same year, she was nominated for a Tony award for her performance in the Broadway play *Look Away*.

In 1975, President Gerald Ford appointed Maya to the American Revolution Bicentennial Council and her

James Baldwin was a black novelist, essayist, and playwright. During the civil rights movement of the 1960s, many people regarded him as a major literary interpreter of the struggles of black Americans.

poetry book *Oh Pray My Wings Are Gonna Fit Me Well* was published. She became a Rockefeller Foundation scholar and spent November and December 1975 at the Bellagio Study and Conference Center on Lake Como in Italy. That same year, she was elected to the Board of Trustees of the American Film Library.

In 1976, Maya received an honorary doctorate degree from the University of Kansas in Lawrence. That same year, 48-year-old Maya wrote two television specials on African-American life and completed her book *Singin' and Swingin' and Gettin' Merry Like Christmas,* which she had begun in Italy. This book covered her life in San Francisco from the time she worked in the record shop and met her first husband, Tosh Angelos, until the time she returned from the traveling tour in Europe with the musical cast of *Porgy and Bess.*

While she had been on that extended European tour, Maya had written long letters to her mother, each letter giving detailed descriptions of whom Maya met and what she did and saw. After *Singin' and Swingin' and Gettin' Merry Like Christmas* was published, Mother took out the letters from long before and reread them. She discovered that Maya had remembered the people, places, and events exactly as they had happened years earlier.

Amidst all her personal and professional triumphs, Maya reluctantly decided to revisit Stamps, Arkansas. The trip was part of a promise made to two media friends—correspondent Bill Moyers and Willie Morris

Diahann Carroll portrayed Maya's mother and John M. Driver II played her brother, Bailey, in a television movie version of I Know Why the Caged Bird Sings, left. Esther Rolle portrayed Maya's grandmother, Momma Annie, below.

of *Harper's* magazine—years before. All three had Southern roots. "I was afraid to go to Arkansas because of demons and I was afraid to look creativity in the eye," she stated. It turned out to be a powerfully emotional journey. In Stamps, many residents came to see her, sharing their remembrances of the town, the Store, Momma Annie, Maya, and Uncle Willie. She met people who had been influenced by her late Uncle Willie's patience and his emphasis on teaching and learning. Maya had come full circle.

And Still I Rise, another volume of poetry, was published in 1978. Her next book, *The Heart of a Woman*, dedicated to her grandson, was published in 1981.

Maya Angelou responding to a question during a 1978 interview in her home

This book, part of Maya's continuing autobiographical series, covers her life from the Sausalito, California, commune to her entrance into Ghanaian society.

Maya is often asked how she designs and writes a book. She explains that each book project begins with a definite idea. The finished concept, however, may turn out to be entirely different. Initially, Maya goes to the small hotel room she rents in order to write without interruption. She begins by writing about her subject in longhand on yellow, lined legal pads. Once this is done and a project begins to take shape, she organizes the material, rewriting it over and over again. Sometimes she reads her work aloud to detect the rhythm of a piece. A finished autobiography may be 600 handwritten pages, which she sends to her editor. Then, ongoing discussions begin.

Maya has stated that no form of writing is easy. Reviewers sometimes call Maya a "natural writer," but that makes her angry. She works diligently at harnessing word power and getting control of language, with the goal of making her readers and listeners feel, weep, or laugh. Sometimes it may take her two days or longer just to get one sentence right. "My responsibility as a writer is to be as good as I can be at my craft," she says.

As Maya gained experience and fame, her marriage to Paul began to erode, and she and Paul separated. They eventually divorced in 1981. Maya later commented that she gave each marriage her very best

Maya spoke at the ninth annual film awards dinner at the National Arts Club.

effort, but if it didn't work, she was brave enough to leave. Paul decided to stay in the San Francisco area. Maya didn't want to see him every place she went, so she moved to North Carolina. She bought a 10-room home, which she expanded to 18 rooms.

In 1982, Maya received a lifetime appointment as Reynolds Professor of American Studies at Wake Forest University in Winston-Salem, North Carolina. The Rare Books Room of the university library contains journals Maya wrote when she was about nine years old. In 1983, when Maya was 55, she received praise for her next poetry collection, *Shaker, Why Don't You Sing?* By then, she was receiving more than 300 fan letters per week.

Maya congratulates her friend Oprah Winfrey, who was awarded a medal at the 1996 International Radio and Television Service Foundation awards dinner.

Maya continues to write, and her busy life includes lectures, television appearances, and travel. Vivacious, witty, and profound on stage, she is reported to be somewhat formal and reserved at home. Maya has talked about the seductiveness of being a celebrity, about the perceived power that comes with it, and about how some people begin to believe their publicity. But she thinks that's dangerous, because instead of being creative, a person begins to imitate his or her past accomplishments. She makes it a point, in order to continually create new works, not to be influenced by the media bonanza that constantly surrounds her.

At 58, Maya completed *All God's Children Need Traveling Shoes,* an autobiographical book about her life in Ghana. *Now Sheba Sings the Song,* a poetry volume, was published in 1987. *I Shall Not Be Moved,* another poetry success, was published in 1990.

By 1991, Maya was also helping to care for her beautiful, beloved, once vivacious mother, who had been diagnosed with cancer. For a while Mother was hooked up to the pale blue wires of an oxygen tank. She died in 1992.

In 1994, Maya received the Horatio Alger Award, which was named after the author she had so loved to read when she was a child. Through the years, Maya had become like one of her early heroes—a poor person who, by hard work and honesty, rose through the ranks of society to positively influence others.

Maya was presented with the 1994 Horatio Alger Award at a luncheon held at the Grand Hyatt Hotel in Washington, D.C.

President Bill Clinton prepares to hug Maya after she recited a poem for his 1993 inauguration. Vice President Al Gore applauds behind the president.

In January 1993, Maya recited "On the Pulse of Morning," the poem she had written for Bill Clinton's presidential inauguration. At the conclusion of her reading, the president embraced Maya on the inaugural platform as the world watched.

That same year, Maya celebrated her 65th birthday. Television talk-show star Oprah Winfrey hosted a party attended by celebrities from all over the world. Winfrey, one of Maya's dearest friends, even designed Maya's dress for the occasion. Maya said, "Oprah is beautiful, tough, and bodacious, the kind of daughter I would have wanted to have." Maya's book *Wouldn't Take Nothing for My Journey Now,* published by

Random House in 1993, is dedicated to Oprah Winfrey "with immeasurable love."

After appearing at the Clinton inauguration, demand
for Maya's time and presence increased even further.
In 1993, her standard fee for appearances was about
$15,000. *My Painted House, My Friendly Chicken and
Me*—a book for young children—was published in
1994, and *The Complete Collected Poems of Maya
Angelou* came out in 1995. That same year Maya
starred in the well-received movie *How to Make an
American Quilt,* playing a character named Anna.

About once a year, Maya permits herself a full day

From left to right, **Maya Angelou, Winona Ryder, and Ellen
Burstyn** in the movie How to Make an American Quilt

Maya sautés some onions and peppers in the kitchen of the Sugar Bar restaurant in New York on September 29, 1997. She spent the day cooking as a guest chef for a benefit dinner to be held that evening.

away from writing, public appearances, and the attention of her worldwide fans. She tells friends and family that she is unavailable and shuts off the phone. On that day, she takes a long walk, wandering streets, looking at buildings, window shopping, browsing in libraries. When she returns home, she sees problems with a new clarity and has a better idea about the projects she wants to tackle next. As her grandmother Annie "Momma" Henderson used to say, when you don't like a thing, change it, and if "you can't change

Maya with her mother, Vivian Baxter

it, change the way you think about it. Don't complain."

Maya receives at least 400–500 fan letters per week, and she lectures to packed audiences. Sometimes she dances on the lecture stage, sometimes she acts out a problem and solution. Noted for the diversity of her talents and successes, Maya has said many times that she thinks of life as an ongoing adventure. Like her autobiographical books, her lectures conclude on an uplifting note of hope. Life will give you experiences, she has often remarked, and these experiences may not always be pleasant, but "Nobody promised you a rose garden. But more than likely if you do dare, what you get are the marvelous returns."

In a commencement speech at the University of Delaware in 1996, Maya told the students they truly had the "ability to be rainbows in the clouds."

Maya Angelou at a New York book signing for Even the Stars Look Lonesome

SOURCES

8   Gayle Pollard Terry, "Maya Angelou: Creating a Poem to Honor a Nation," *Los Angeles Times*, January 20, 1993.

11   Maya Angelou, *I Know Why the Caged Bird Sings* (New York: Bantam Books, 1993), 68.

12   Ibid., 5.

16   Ibid., 22.

19   Jeffrey M. Elliot, ed., *Conversations with Maya Angelou* (Jackson, Mississippi: University Press of Mississippi, 1989), 4.

21   Angelou, *I Know Why the Caged Bird Sings*, 26.

21   Ibid., 28.

24   Ibid., 58.

24   Ibid., 3.

26–27   Ibid., 72.

27   Ibid., 80.

30   Catherine Manegold, "A Wordsmith at Her Inaugural Anvil, *The New York Times*, January 20, 1993.

31   Howard Chua-Eoan, "Moment of Creation," *People*, January 18, 1993, 62.

31   Jessie Carney Smith, ed., *Notable Black American Women* (Detroit: Gale Research, 1992).

36   Maya Angelou, *Even the Stars Look Lonesome* (New York: Random House, 1997), 130.

37   Distinguished Annie Clark Tanner Lecture, Weber State University, May 8, 1997.

38   Angelou, *I Know Why the Caged Bird Sings*, 26.

38   Ibid.

39   Ibid., 179.

40   http:/www.olympics/zccl36c.htc (quoting Das Schwarze Korps, undated).

41   Angelou, *I Know Why the Caged Bird Sings*, 180.

41   Ibid., 181.

42   Ibid., 183.

42   Ibid., 184.

46   Elliot, 4.
48   Angelou, *I Know Why the Caged Bird Sings,* 217.
49   Ibid., 245.
51   Ibid., 265.
56   Maya Angelou, *Gather Together in My Name* (New York: Bantam Books, 1993), 50.
56   Ibid., 61.
64   Ibid., 160.
73   Maya Angelou, *Singin' and Swingin' and Gettin' Merry Like Christmas* (New York: Bantam Books, 1977), 238.
78   Elliot, 57.
87   Maya Angelou, *The Heart of a Woman* (New York: Bantam Books, 1993), 271.
96   Jacqueline Trescott, "Maya Angelou's Pressure-Cooker Poem," *Washington Post,* January 16, 1993.
97   Elliot, 59.
97   Ibid., 149.
101   "Oprah Throws a Party," *Ebony,* June 1993, 118–120.
102   Maya Angelou, *Wouldn't Take Nothing for My Journey Now* (New York: Bantam Books, 1994), dedication.
103–104   Ibid., 87.
105   Elliot, 85.
105   Maya Angelou, University of Delaware commencement speech, June 6, 1996.

BIBLIOGRAPHY

Angelou, Maya. *All God's Children Need Traveling Shoes.* New York: Vintage Books, 1991.

_____. *Even the Stars Look Lonesome.* New York: Random House, 1997.

_____. *Gather Together in My Name.* New York: Bantam Books, 1993.

_____. *I Know Why the Caged Bird Sings.* New York: Bantam Books, 1993.

_____. *Singin' and Swingin' and Gettin' Merry Like Christmas.*

New York: Bantam Books, 1977.

———. *The Complete Collected Poems of Maya Angelou*. New York: Random House, 1994.

———. *The Heart of a Woman*. New York: Bantam, 1993.

———. *Wouldn't Take Nothing for My Journey Now*. New York: Bantam Books, 1994.

Benson, Carol. "Out of the Cage and Still Singing," *Writer's Digest*, 1975, 19-21.

Bloom, Harold, ed. *Black American Women Fiction Writers*. New York: Chelsea House Publishers, 1995.

Bredeson, Carmen. *American Writers of the 20th Century*. New Jersey: Enslow Publishers, 1996.

Brown, Ray B., ed. *Contemporary Heroes and Heroines*. New York: Gale Research, 1990.

Chua-Eoan. Howard. "Moment of Creation," *People*, January 18, 1993, 62.

"Education," *Jet*, July 11, 1994, 20.

Elliot, Jeffrey M., ed. *Conversations with Maya Angelou*. Jackson: University Press of Mississippi, 1989.

Graham, Judith, ed. *Current Biography Yearbook*. New York: H. W. Wilson Co., 1994.

Hagen, Lyman B. *Heart of a Woman, Mind of a Writer, and Soul of a Poet*. New York: University Press of America, 1997.

International Who's Who. England: Europa Publications, 1993-4

Jennings, Peter & David Brinkley. Inauguration Video, ABC News, 1993.

Kranz, Rachel. "Black Americans." *Facts on File*. New York: Facts on File, 1992.

Lambert, Paul. "Chapter and Verse." *People*, October 3, 1994, 108–110.

Manegold, Catherine. "A Wordsmith at Her Inaugural Anvil," *New York Times*, January 20, 1993.

Meroney, John. "The Real Maya Angelou." *American Spectator*, March 1993, 68.

Moritz, Charles, ed., *Current Biography*. New York: H. W. Wilson Co., 1974.

New Lincoln Library Encyclopedia, vol. 3. Columbus, Ohio: Frontier Press Company, 1981.

"Oprah Throws a Party," *Ebony*, June 1993, 118–120.

Smith, Jessie Carney, ed. *Notable Black American Women.* Detroit: Gale Research, 1992.

Smith, Sande, ed. *Who's Who in African-American History.* New York: Smithmark Publishers, 1994.

Spradling, Mary Mace, ed. *In Black and White.* Detroit: Gale Research, 1980.

Terry, Gayle Pollard. "Maya Angelou, Creating a Poem to Honor a Nation." *Los Angeles Times,* January 20, 1993.

"This Week in Black History," *Jet,* May 13, 1995, 20.

Trescott, Jacqueline. "Maya Angelou's Pressure-Cooker Poem." *Washington Post,* January 16, 1993.

Trosky, Susan M, ed. Detroit: Gale Research, 1994.

Urdang, Laurence, ed. *The Time Tables of American History.* New York: Simon & Schuster, 1981.

Who's Who? New York: St. Martin's Press, 1997.

WEB: MAYA ANGELOU SITES

Brandes, Maya. Maya Angelou, A Bibliography of Literary Criticism.

Distinguished Annie Clark Tanner Lecture, Weber State University, May 8, 1997.

Frost, David. An Interview with Maya Angelou, 1995.

The Clinton Inauguration, WH/Family/html/Inauguration.

University of Delaware Commencement Ceremony speech by Maya Angelou, June 6, 1996.

INDEX

ABOUT THE AUTHOR

L. Patricia "Pat" Kite is an award-winning children's book author. She has a special love for research—especially in the fields of biology and biography. Kite holds a teaching credential in biology and social science and a master's degree in journalism. She is a New York native but has spent the last 30 years in Newark, California, where she raised four children as a single parent. Kite's hobbies include gardening, reading, distance walking, local politics, and volunteer work.

PHOTO ACKNOWLEDGMENTS

AP/Wide World Photos, 6, 39, 50, 78, 79, 84, 88, 93, 101, 103; Archive Photos, 22, 96; Corbis-Bettmann, 18, 42; Frank Driggs/Corbis-Bettmann, 48; © M. Gerber/Corbis, 99; © Henry McGee/Globe Photos, Inc., 98; © James M. Kelly/Globe Photos, Inc., 100; Karen J. Kite, 112; Library of Congress, 66; Mary Ellen Mark, 9, 58, 91, 104; Dr. Deborah Pellow, 86; Photofest, 72, 95 (both); © Nancy Robinson, 2; Schomburg Center for Research in Black Culture, 32, 34, 35 [Marion Post, 10, 17], [Russell Lee, 14, 19]; © Mike Schreiber/Retna Ltd. Inc., 105; © Douglas Steakley, 44; Suzanne Tenner/Fotos, 102; UPI/Corbis-Bettmann, 16, 28, 36, 38, 74, 76, 83; Wisconsin Center for Film and Theater Research, 82.

Front cover, © M. Gerber/Corbis; back cover, AP/Wide World Photos